The Descendants of James McNamee

DAVID MCNAMEE, PH.D.

DEDICATION

This book is humbly dedicated to the people whose names are chronicled within these pages. Your stories should have been told and preserved long before I came along.

I'm extremely grateful to my sister, Barbara Jean McNamee (Wilson), and Aunt Charlotte Maree (McNamee) Leipold for reading the draft of this book and catching my mistakes and adding their own memories to the life stories of the McNamee family. I am also thankful for my patient wife, Lynne, who encouraged me to get out and visit some of the places that the McNamee's called home.

Most important, this book is dedicated to my Dad, Bobby Deane McNamee.

1 INTRODUCTION

This book was in the works for quite a while. Shortly after my father, Bobby Deane McNamee, passed away just shy of his 51st birthday I began to think that I should have paid more attention to the stories being told around the Ping Pong table that served as the family dining table whenever the family got together in Grandpa John Gallucci's basement in Portland, OR. The idea of this book seriously took root not long after the birth of our first son. At first vaguely, later more concretely, I realized that someday my children or grandchildren might want to know something of their family history. As time marched forward and more and more relatives (and sources of information) passed on with their stories untold, this book became really needed.

Truth be told, I need this book as much as anyone. Growing up as the eldest son of a U.S. Air Force Senior Non-Commissioned Officer who spent his career travelling the world in service to his country, I often felt a profound sense of rootlessness; a sense of not quite "belonging" to wherever it was we were living at the time. Even now, though we've lived in Oregon for over two decades, if someone asks, "Where are you from?" I must pause and think about what answer is most appropriate. If someone says, "tell me about your family," I can only respond by saying, "Well...I'm not really sure."

This book, then, is an attempt to answer those two questions. It is not meant to be the whole answer. Nor is this meant to be the definitive history of this branch of the McNamee family. I am certain I have made mistakes. For those mistakes or omissions, I take full responsibility and ask for a measure of grace and understanding. The goal of this book is to simply capture what I do know or what I have been able to unearth in the process of research up to this point in time. My hope is that this is the beginning of a conversation that will go on for many generations.

Some words about focus, style and sources: The first part of this book comes from my research into the origins of the McNamee family name. Most of that research took place in the Spring of 2017 as Lynne and I prepared for a month-long stay in Ireland and Scotland. During the trip in the summer of 2017, I gathered much information from the Public Records Office of Northern Ireland (PRONI) located in Belfast, the General Register Office (GRO) and the National Archives of Ireland, both located in Dublin, the Irish Family History Centre and EPIC The Irish Emigration Museum of Dublin. The Mellon Centre for Migration Studies in Ulster provided information specific to migration and emigration from the Ulster area and generously shared an unpublished document specifically talking about the McNamee family seat and the relationship of the McNamee's to the ruling O'Neil clan.

The second part of this story mostly takes place in Missouri and Nebraska where the family of Michael McNamee finally put down roots. Background research consisted mostly of reading digitized copies of newspapers published by the *Ord Quiz* as well as other newspapers and an old copy of published histories. The software used to compile this information is Family Tree Maker, which I've been using since it first came out on "floppy disks." The online version of this family tree may be found at Ancestry.com. This book would not be possible without the hints provided by Ancestry's little wiggling leaves. Lastly, my research included trips to Wyoming and Missouri to wander through cemeteries and visit the Wyoming State Archives. I've made note of those sources wherever appropriate.

In both parts of the book, I've attempted to accurately portray the facts as I've found them. Because so much of what can be found "out there" is inaccurate, misleading hearsay, I paid particular attention to ensuring that everything here is supported by credible sources. But I wanted more than just a dry research report. I wanted to capture a sense of the world in which the McNamee family lived, loved, worked, played, and died. To that end, I've tried to weave a narrative that is accurate, revealing and enjoyable.

The focus of this book is rather narrow. My first goal was to learn and share as much as possible about Michael and Anna Mary McNamee and their eleven children. In order to keep the project manageable, I included some information about spouses but decided to leave information about children for future books. My second goal was to attempt to link Michael back to Ireland: to learn who his parents were; where he came from in Ireland (family lore said Belfast, but there was no firm evidence to support the story); and gain a sense of what life might have been like for the McNamee's back in "the old country." In this second task, I failed. Not for lack of trying, mind you, but simply because the documented facts weren't enough to make that link back to the old country. Thus, that remains a goal for future researchers or maybe a future edition of this book. One surprise expanded the scope of this book slightly. Discovering that Michael's father was not another Michael, but a James McNamee changed the entire focus of my efforts to link the McNamee's back to Ireland.

So, let's begin.

2 ORIGINS OF THE MCNAMEE NAME

Names tie us to each other. Names also tie us to places and give us roots, meaning, even self-identity. Everyone recognizes himself or herself by name. It's often the first thing we learn about ourselves as our mothers whisper our names to us. Names hint at culture. Very often the first piece of information we have about another person is their name. The power of a name and its value has long been immortalized in prose, poetry, and religious ceremony. Author Patrick Rothfuss, penned an interesting fiction book series based on the premise that to know "the name of all things" meant that "all things were his to command." And so, we begin by asking about the origin of the name, McNamee.

Noted researcher and one of the foremost genealogists of twentieth century Ireland, Edward MacLysaght noted that:

"Ireland was one of the earliest countries to evolve a system of hereditary surnames. They came into being fairly generally in the eleventh century, and indeed a few were formed before the year 1000."

Why? As the Irish population grew, something beyond a simple single name was needed to help people know not only who someone was, but also who they were in relation to family, clan, or tribe. Surnames helped others understand whether you were someone of means and power or whether you were merely a follower or servant. Surnames might say something about your family's traditional occupation, baker, for example. Surnames might even capture some sense of a person's character or a family trait; *Mac Dubhghaill*, for example originally referred to "black stranger" but in modern times, refers to MacDowell. Surnames also helped identify particular individuals to the tax collectors.

In the next few pages, you will see that two names—the O'Neill's and the McNamee's have been tied to each other since ancient times.

O'Neill. From the *Annals of the Four Masters* we are given an account of the rise of one of the great kings of Ireland. *Niall Noígíallach* or in English, Niall of the Nine Hostages, was an Irish king who is said to have reigned over Ireland between the late 4th and early 5th centuries. Niall is the ancestor of the Uí Néill family that dominated Ireland from the 6th to the 10th century (see illustrated map).

The Ui Neill family (in modern times this became O'Neill) divided into two "over-kingdoms," the Northern Uí Néill, which controlled north-western medieval Ireland, and the Southern Uí Néill, which controlled central and eastern Ireland. As we shall see later, the McNamee clan originated within the boundaries of the Southern Ui Neill but ended up serving the Northern Ui Neills.

A note about the *Annals of the Four Masters*: The *Annals of the Kingdom of Ireland* or the *Annals of the Four Masters* are a collection of chronicles of medieval Irish history. The entries span from the Deluge, dated as 2,242 years after creation to AD 1616. They were compiled between 1632 and 1636 from several sources, earlier chronicles, and some original research under the patronage of a Gaelic lord and serve as a principal source of information about Irish history. Written in Gaelic, several well-translated and edited versions are available online for future researchers. An original copy of the manuscript is kept on display at Trinity College in Dublin, Ireland; a grand old university that Lynne and I were privileged to visit in 2017. At least four Mac Conmidhe's or MacNamee's have entries in the Annals.

The O'Neill Lordship. In his book *Gallon*, William John Bradley noted that

"Gaelic civilization flourished in Ireland for several centuries in spite of the fierce rivalries between provincial kings and the frequent threat of external invasion. However, unlike most other countries of Europe, Gaelic Ireland never achieved lasting unity under a single monarchy, making the country more vulnerable to conquest by ambitious foreigners."

Members of the O'Neill family ruled the territory of Tir Owen from the middle of the 13th century until the Plantation of Ulster in the early 17th century. The territory of Tir Owen occupied the counties of Tyrone, Armagh, Down, Antrim, Londonderry and northwest Donegal and Argyll in Scotland (The yellow area of the map on next page). This was later referred to as the Province of Ulster.

Men of learning and culture were highly esteemed by the O'Neills. The McNamee's were the official poets to the O'Neills, and one of them, Tadhg, had his own castle at Lough Mary (near present day Newtown Stewart) in the 15th century. According to Bradley, the O'Neills were noted for their great hospitality and in Brian MacAngus McNamee, they had a noted bard. They held their bardic festival annually and welcomed guests from all over Ireland. Traditionally they held this event around Christmas.

Mac Con Midhe. The name translates literally as Mac (Son of) Con (the hound) Midhe (Meath). According to the *Dictionary of American Family Names*, McNamee is the Anglicized form of the Gaelic name *Mac Conmidhe*, which in turn is a patronymic (a name derived from the name of a father or male ancestor) from the personal name Cú Mhidhe, meaning 'hound of Meath'. This family were hereditary poets in Ulster.

According to one source, the McNamee name first appears in County Westmeath, a part of the Midlands Region. Westmeath is named after the ancient Kingdom of Meath (Gaelic: *Mide*) (see map).

The Revered James O'Laverty, author of *An Historical Account of the Diocese of Down and Connor, Ancient and Modern, Volume 1* (published in Dublin in 1878) noted this about the McNamee's:

"The MacNamees were originally chiefs of the Sil-Ronan, a tribe situated along Lough Ree, in West Meath, hence they derived their name from some of their ancestors called Cu Midhe—the hound of Meath. The Irish, who had not lions in their country, compared their chiefs to the hound, the animal which they held in highest esteem…A branch of the MacNamees became hereditary poets to the Kinel-Owen. Dr. O'Donovan states that the late Mr. Loughlin MacNamee, of Ballynascreen, County Derry, was the lineal representative of Solamh MacNamee, chief poet of O'Neill, who died in 1507."

Why Hound of Meath? Looking through the *Irish Book of Names*, it became clear that the reference is complimentary. Referring to someone as "the hound of…" is another way to call them "warrior" or "defender" or "hero" of something or someone. We see this in the story of an early Irish hero named Cu (or Con) Chulainn. CuChulain, whose birth name was Setanta, was given his adult name after he killed a ferocious Irish wolfhound watch dog that belonged to the local blacksmith. The blacksmith had invited Setanta to a party he was giving for the king. To protect the king while he was at the party, the blacksmith had put his watchdog on guard outside the house. Setanta, who at 17 was able to out-wrestle and outplay 150 other youths, was challenged by the watch dog. Setanta, not knowing to whom the wolfhound belonged threw his ball at the hound so hard that it went through the hound's mouth and "carried the guts within him out through his back door."

Upon finding out that he had mistakenly killed a valuable hound, Setanta, agreed to assume the dog's place and duties until another wolfhound could be raised and trained. He was renamed Cu Chulainn "hound of Culann." Cu Chulainn went on to perform other famous deeds which were gathered together in epic story.

From this story, we begin to see the why being called "The Hound of Meath" is a good thing. In this case, Mac Con Midhe refers to The Son of the Defender or Warrior of County Meath. Other early names that begin with cu are Cu Maige (Hound of the Plain); Cu Mara (Hound of the Sea); and Cu Coigriche (Hound of the Border).

Septs, Clans, Seats, Tribes and Family Crests. **Sept** is a term that refers to a division or branch of a particular **family** or **clan**. There may be several septs within a clan. Septs and clans may be part of an even larger group called a **tribe**.

Though the McNamee clan has many famous people in it, including a few well-bred minor nobility, **there is no official family crest**. Because the McNamee's were retainers or followers of the O'Neill's, any crests that they may have displayed were very likely to be the O'Neill family crest. Don't waste your money buying them online...unless you just happen to like them. The McNamee clan is listed as one of ten clans united under the royal Clan Neill whose hereditary Chief was Ua Néill Ruadh, also known as Ó Néill Mór (O'Neill). It was known by several spellings of the name, including Mac Conmidhe (MacNAMEE, MacCONAMY, MacMEADH, MEE).

The original McNamee clan, which had several septs or branches, was Ulster-based and were close followers of the O'Neills, the principal rulers of Northern Ireland, and they suffered with the O'Neills in their support of the Catholic King James II of England and Ireland. Brian Mac Angus MacNamee was chief poet to Luineach O'Neill, and died in 1595. Among the many name holders of considerable importance was Teige oge MacConmea of Neadenurry, County Clare, who died in 1602, and Charles MacNamee in the muster of regimental officers in the army of King James in 1689. There was a branch of the Ulster sept who were erenaghs (people responsible for receiving parish revenue from tithes and rents, building and maintaining church property and overseeing the tenant lands that generated parish income) of Comber on the river Foyle in the deanery of Derry. (A deanery is an ecclesiastical entity in the Roman Catholic Church or the Church of England; a church's jurisdiction, if you will.)

The first recorded spelling of the family name is that of Gilla Bridghe Mac Con Midhe, which was dated 1260 in the annals of the poets of Ireland, during the reign of King Henry III of England, 1216 - 1272. *The genealogy of Corca Laidhe* in *Miscellany of the Celtic Society,* (first published in 1849, and written by John O'Donovan) said that

"Gilla Bhrighde Mac Conmidhe (or Gilbride Mac Namee) was chief poet of Ulster in his time, and the friend and follower of Brian O'Neill, King of the Irish of the North, and Righdhamhna or heir presumptive to the throne of Ireland. The family of Mac Conmidhe, of which this Gilla-Bhrighde was the head, were hereditary poets to the northern Ui-Neill,

and are still very numerous in Ulster. Maelseachlainn Mac Conmidhe (Loughlin Mac Namee) of Draperstown Cross in the County of Derry, was believed to be the head of this family in 1835."

Some sources state that the McNamee family seat is in Meath or West Meath. There is no definitive proof that this is so. What is clear is that the McNamee's came from West Meath.

About 1606 the Ulster Plantation records show McNamee's among the natives of County Tyrone and later in the century the name appeared in Charles O'Neill's regiment in James II's Irish army. Tyrone and Derry is where the name is mainly found today. During our visit to the Mellon Centre for Migration Studies in the summer of 2017, I spoke with Ann Duffy, Heritage Services Manager, about the origin of the McNamee clan. She, in turn, put me in touch with William John Bradley, author of *Gallon: The History of Three Townlands in County Tyrone from the Earliest Times to the Present Day* (published by Guildhall Press in 2000). Dr. Bradley assured me that it is safe to assume that the **Family Seat for the McNamee family was located near Lough Mary, which is part of the Baronscourt Estate, near Newtown Stewart, in County Tyrone.** On the map, the approximate location is marked with a star.

Genetic Footprints or Games of Thrones. With the growing popularity of

DNA testing, it might be interesting to note that the McNamee clan may be more than associated with the O'Neills. Based on the results of DNA I've had tested by FamilyTreeDNA (the original DNA matching program) and Ancestry DNA, we are actually distant cousins!

A study, published in the *American Journal of Human Genetics*, that was conducted at Trinity College Dublin, Ireland found that a striking percentage of men in Ireland (and quite a few in Scotland) share the same Y chromosome, suggesting that the 5th-century warlord known as "Niall of the Nine Hostages" may be the ancestor of one-in-12 Irishmen. Niall established a dynasty of powerful chieftains that dominated the island for six centuries. My Y chromosome matches the profile!

In the study scientists found an area in northwest Ireland where they claim 21.5% carry Niall's genetic fingerprint. This area was the main powerbase of the Ui Neills, which literally translated means "descendants of Niall." The study said the Y chromosome appeared to trace back to one person. The study author said, *"As in other polygynous societies, the siring of offspring was related to power and prestige."* The study mentions that just one of the O'Neill dynasty chieftains who died in 1423 had 18 sons with nearly a dozen women and claimed 59 grandsons.

Niall of the Nine Hostages received his name from the taking of hostages as a strategy for playing mental havoc upon his opponent chieftains. He is known in folklore as a raider of the British and French coasts. Supposedly slain in the English Channel or in Scotland, his descendants were the most powerful rulers of Ireland until the 11th century.

Celtic Legacy: Where Our Story Begins. "Who am I?" is a question all of us ask at some time in our lives. As we search for the answer, we begin to define ourselves. Many factors shape our answer to the question, "Who am I?" including where we are from. How does our location shape who we are and what we believe? How does the physical environment impact what we do and how we behave? How does our location relative to other places

influence our ideas about difference band our relationships with others?

Though we are far removed in both time and distance from the place which the McNamee's called home, it still strikes me as important to at least have a sense of the place that originally shaped our ancestors. In a sense, this chapter paints a broad backdrop for understanding their life and their times.

County Meath. The kingdom of Midhe (or Meath) emerged from the mists in the first century CE as one of the five kingdoms established by the Insular Celts who inhabited Ireland. The other four kingdoms were: Ulster, Connaught, Leinster, and Munster. In his book, *Celts: A Dark History*, Martin J. Dougherty points out that the Celts were a "mysterious people whose history is shrouded in myth and misinformation." A fascinating read, *Celts* also makes clear that the Celtic people were singularly responsible for much

of the language, beliefs, and the very fabric of modern Ireland. The kingdom of Midhe is particularly important because its territory includes the hill of Tara, which had mythological significance as well as being the seat of the High Kings of Ireland. For all of the Tolkien fans in the family, Midhe (in Gaelic midhe means middle) is quite literally the middle kingdom!

The day was blustery and cold as Lynne and I walked around the Hill of Tara. As our young tour guide told stories of Irish Celtic kings, it was not hard to imagine an early McNamee standing where we stood, taking note of what his king said and later recording it in local chronicles. The Stone of Destiny (see the photo) was the inauguration stone for these Kings. One hundred and forty-two Kings are said to have reigned in the name of Tara and legend has it that when the Stone of Destiny is touched by a true King it will cry out! In ancient Irish religion and mythology Temair or Tara was the sacred place of dwelling for the gods and was the entrance to the otherworld. Saint Patrick is said to have come to Tara to confront the ancient religion of the pagans at its most powerful site.

One interpretation of the name Tara says that it means a "place of great prospect" and I can only imagine the view our poetic McNamee ancestors had on clear days when it is possible to see features in half the counties of Ireland. Northwest of Tara is the brilliant white quartz front of

Newgrange and further north lies the Hill of Slane, where according to legend St. Patrick lit his Pascal fire prior to his visit to Tara in 433 AD.

County Tyrone. Tyrone was a kingdom of Gaelic Ireland, associated geographically with present-day County Tyrone, County Armagh, and parts of County Londonderry/Derry. Tyrone was the traditional stronghold of the various O'Neill clans and families, the strongest of the Gaelic Irish families in Ulster, surviving into the seventeenth century. In the map on the previous page, the center of the area entitled "The Great O'Neill" was the area the McNamee's called home. Today, that area is on the border between County Tyrone and County Derry (Map p. 8).

Historian William John Bradley noted that "members of the O'Neill family ruled the territory of Tir Owen (Tyrone) from the middle of the thirteenth century until the Plantation of Ulster in the early seventeenth century." One of the most notable local kings was Henry Aimhreidh (Harry Avery) O'Neill who, according to local folklore, built his castle in a commanding position overlooking the southern end of the Mourne valley around 1360. The ruins of this castle are a well-known landmark on a hill just outside Newtownstewart. (see photo below) About 200 years and two miles away, another O'Neill built another castle beside the river Mourne to guard a strategic crossing place. Over time, a settlement grew up there which became known as Lisglas or Baile Nua (Newtown) which even later became Newtownstewart. Somewhere in the vicinity is the seat of the McNamee clan. Life for the McNamee clan would have been very different from today. Very likely those not employed by the O'Neill's as poets or ollavs, would have

been farmers or worked in the linen industry that was the mainstay of Ireland's economy in the 16th century. Bradley described it this way:

Apart from the ancient road which followed the rivers Strule and Mourne, there were very few roads in Tir Owen in the 16th century. Travelers depended on tracks and also used boats to travel on the deeper rivers. Towns were few in number and seldom consisted of more than a few houses. Most families lived in little circular post-and-wattle houses. There was no chimney; the fire was lit in the middle of the floor and the smoke escaped through a hole in the centre of the roof. (see photo below)

Livestock, especially cattle, were the main source and manifestation of wealth for lords and clan members alike. The clan members owned few cattle and looked after other cattle for their lord.

In the valleys, small enclosures close to the home settlements were fenced off to grow oats, barley, flax and vegetables. Oats were ground by hand or in the local mill and flax was spun into linen to make tunics. Pigs and sheep were fattened for meat and the wool was woven into cloth to make a thick woolen cloak known as the Irish mantle.

Woods were plentiful in the valleys. A wide range of wild animals such as the elk, deer, hare, and wolf lived in the woods. Diets were supplemented with salmon and trout.

3 COMING TO AMERICA

We may never know why the McNamee's came to America. The Great Famine (1845-1849) may have been an indirect influence as the economic hardships created by the famine led to Irish emigrants being scattered around the globe. Today there are over 5 million people in Ireland, while it is estimated there are upwards of 70 million people of Irish descent throughout the world. (Source: Rootsweb "Ireland's History in Maps"). The end of the American Civil War (1861 – 1865) opened a new era of expansion and industrialization that attracted Irish immigrants. The first documented date of arrival for our Michael McNamee was 1866 although there is a hint that his father James McNamee may have been in America even earlier. It was common for one member of the family to arrive early and arrange for others to follow. Lastly, the arrival of the McNamee's may have been influenced by religious differences. The Irish Troubles of the 1960s – 1990s have their roots in the centuries old tension between the Protestants and Catholics of Ireland. Even today, as we experienced during our 2017 visit to Ireland, tensions simmer just under the surface of conversations and relations. It is interesting to note that in the Census of 1930, Michael McNamee lists himself and his mother as coming from Northern Ireland (which is largely Protestant) while his father James was listed as having roots in the Irish Free State (which is by-and-large Catholic or Anglican). America's reputation for religious tolerance would have been attractive. Whatever the motivation, the McNamee family came to America circa 1866.

Arrival. Immigrants to America often relied on the largesse of family members who preceded them to provide tickets and passage.

Castle Clinton, also referred to as Castle Garden, is a fort and national monument located in Battery Park at the southern tip of Manhattan in New York City. The structure has served as a fort, theater, opera house, national immigrant receiving station, and aquarium throughout its long history. Today, Castle Garden is called Castle Clinton National Monument and serves as the ticket center for ferries to Ellis Island and the Statue of Liberty.

Castle Garden. Castle Clinton began its interesting life as a fort built to defend New York Harbor from the British during the War of 1812. Twelve years after the war it was ceded to New York City by the U.S. Army. The former fort reopened in 1824 as Castle Garden, a public cultural center and theatre. In 1855, Castle Garden became America's first immigrant receiving center, welcoming more than 8 million immigrants before it was closed on

April 18, 1890. Castle Garden was succeeded by Ellis Island in 1892.

We don't know yet whether the McNamee's landed at Ellis Island, Castle Clinton, or somewhere else. Other common points of entry included Boston and Philadelphia. A final port of entry that was used by many McNamee's was New Orleans, Louisiana. This is because St. Louis, Missouri, which straddles the mighty Mississippi River, had a reputation as "Little Ireland" and attracted several groups of the larger McNamee clan. There is interesting evidence that our McNamee's may have entered through Canada or Nova Scotia. Time and research will tell. As to when the McNamee's arrived, Census reports offer conflicting information. 1866 is the year mentioned most frequently in family stories. However, the 1920 and 1930 Census both mention 1867 and data from the 1880 Census suggests possibilities in 1862 and 1864.

4 THE SETTING

Before we launch into learning about the members of the McNamee family, it is helpful to understand a bit about that land that beckoned them westward.

First Stop: Lexington, Kentucky. Michael McNamee's obituary in the *Ord Quiz* tells us that the McNamee family's first stop was in Lexington, Kentucky. Bennett Henderson Young's book, *"A history of Jessamine County, Kentucky, from its earliest settlement to 1898"* described Nicholasville, a small town in Jessamine County and today a suburb of Lexington, as achieving local prominence when the Kentucky Central Railroad finally came through in 1857. While the town claims to have "planted the first vineyards west of the Alleghanies" in 1796, the wine industry was largely a dismal failure. The town's charter dutifully noted a population of 49 dogs and the town's company of state militia was locally known as the "Corn Stalk Militia" because there were no arms for the troops who frequently trained with corn stalks instead of rifles.

In the late 1870s-1880s, when the McNamee family likely arrived, the town boasted of nine major businesses, two newspapers, two large grain mills, a hemp manufacturer, a livery stable, and a handful of churches of various denominations. The railyard posted annual revenues of $25,000 worth of freight and $3,000 worth of passengers.

Second Stop: Richmond, Ray County, Missouri. Richmond was founded in 1827 as the county seat of Ray County, Missouri. Richmond was founded, 1827, as the seat of Ray County on land donated by John Wollard, W. B. Martin, and Isaac and William Thornton. The county, organized 1820, had its first seat at Bluffton, where Camden, an early Missouri River port, was laid out. Richmond is located just 40 miles east of downtown Kansas City, Mo. and is in 2017 home to 5,797 residents.

Ray COUNTY COURTHOUSE 2019.
pHOTO BY dAVID mCnAMEE

The "*History of Ray County, MO*" was published by the St. Louis, Missouri Historical Society in 1881. What follows is a beautiful description from that book of what the first settlers in Ray County saw:

The first settlers within the boundaries afterwards embracing Ray county, came in the summer of 1815.
The country was not a wilderness, not a dreary waste; it was a broad expanse of diversified area, rich, productive, beautiful; but undeveloped, unpolished by the hand of art, undisturbed in the embrace of nature's God.

The pioneers' old fashioned Virginia wagons, covered with white canvas, drawn by three horses, forming a " spike team," guided by a single line attached to the rein of the leader's bridle, and in the hands of a driver seated on the rear horse at the left wheel, halted on the east bank of Crooked river, not far above its mouth. It was August. The trees were crowned with luxuriant foliage. The forest was resonant with its own music, and redolent of summer's perfume. Spread out before the travel-worn immigrant in all its pristine beauty, nature's handiwork presented a scene too inviting to pass. The opposite was the more attractive shore, but the stream was swollen, and how to cross was a problem to solve. It was quickly done. Trees were felled, a raft made, and the party swimming their horses, passed safe to the other shore, and went into camp. Thus, though its privations continued for a time, a long and toilsome journey, all the way from the sterile hills of East Tennessee, was brought to a welcome ending; and the first white families, who paused to remain, west of Grand river from the Missouri to the Iowa line, passed the first night within what afterwards became the limits of Ray county.

Their tents and canvassed wagons afforded them enough shelter for the summer and early fall, but not from the rigors of winter. Quarters more substantial and capacious had to be built of logs, and ere this work could be completed, autumn's golden glamour was fading in the " sear and yellow leaf." Winter was coming on apace, and soon "The embattled forests, erewhile armed with gold, their banners bright with every martial hue, stood like some sad, beaten host of old, Withdrawn afar in Time's remotest blue."

But their hovels were finished in time to shield them from the severity of winter, and that season was doubtless passed with little suffering and in comparative comfort, considering the proximity of savages and ferocious wild animals.

The place of the first settlements was called Buffalo, probably because frequented by that animal, and was not far from the present site of Hardin, in what is now Crooked River township, in the southeastern part of the county.

By 1881, Richmond had grown into a prosperous small town whose economic engine was driven by 64 businesses of various types. Two papers, the *Richmond Conservator* and the *Richmond Democrat*, competed for readers and advertising. Delmonico's Restaurant advertised a premier dining experience.

The Richmond Opera House and Olympic Hall, both completed in 1880, offered seating for as many as 800 patrons of the arts. The old cemetery had its own claim to fame as the final resting place of Bloody Bill Anderson, a Confederate guerrilla-turned-outlaw, who led a gang of more than 100 desperados that included a lanky, blond 21-year-old Alexander Franklin James, who went by the name of Frank and his 16-year-old brother Jesse. It was served primarily by the St. Joseph branch of the Wabash, St. Louis and Pacific Railway.

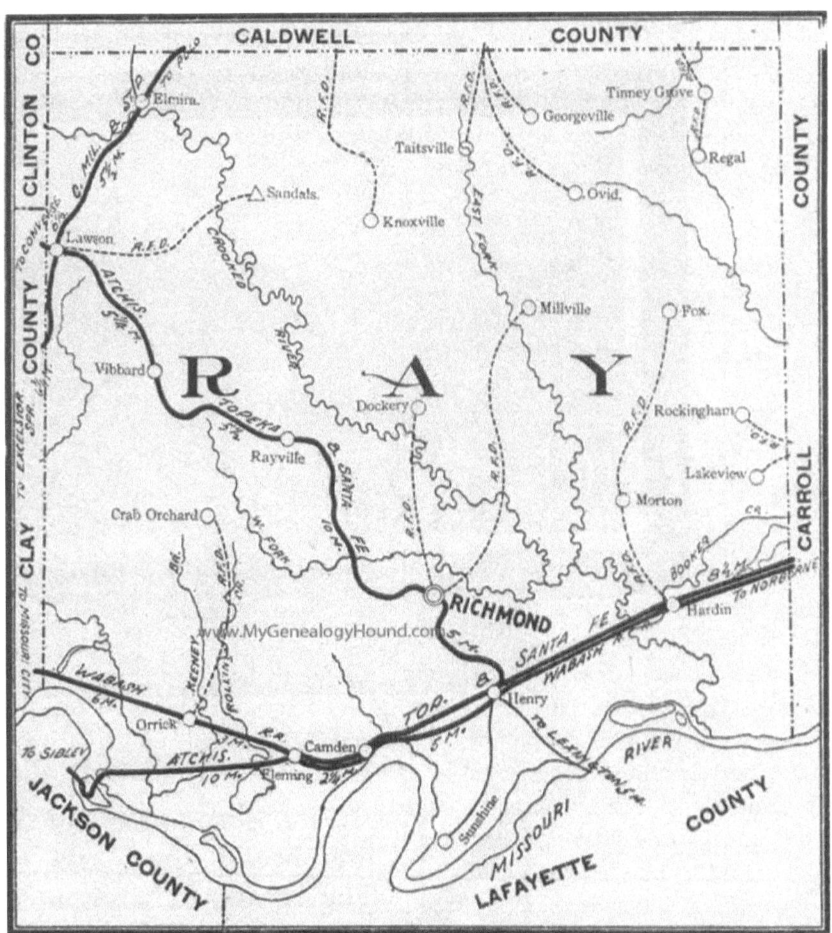

Third Stop: Vinton Township, Valley County, Nebraska. Vinton is a ghost town now. The U. S. Post Office that was established there in 1875 delivered its last letter 1888. H. W. Nelson established a newspaper, the Valley County Courier, in Vinton in 1878 with the hopes of encouraging settlers to populate the town. But Vinton never gained traction and Nelson moved his paper to Ord. On November 18, 1878, the Burlington & Missouri River Railroad Company donated the Vinton town site to the settlers, but the placed never made a town of any great size.

The view in all directions, even today, is of rolling farmland, dotted with the occasional farm. Five miles northeast, Ord, with a population of about 1,200 people, offered access to the railroad and postal service.

An invasion of grasshoppers in the summer of 1874 had devastated millions of acres of crops and forced farmers out of business. But by 1878, crop yields had improved considerably and immigration to Vinton Valley was again in full swing. By June 1, 1880, the population of Vinton County had reached 2,324. By the first of January 1881, it was 3,000 people. By 1882, the population had swelled to 4,000 farmers.

Photo: Homesteaders entering Loup Valley, 1880s, planted wind breaks and established homes in Valley County. [Nebraska State Historical Society]

As travelers drive along the beautiful North Loup River as it winds through the valley in north central Nebraska, they view scenes of breath-taking beauty. The trees, remnants of the early pioneer plantings, provide wind breaks, and the short grasslands on the rougher terrain provide forage for grazing cattle. The wide valleys, formerly areas of native grass, are now carefully measured fields of alfalfa, corn, wheat, and milo. Farm buildings and homes are neatly painted and well-kept. The trails made by migrating Indians are now our paved roads such as state highways 11 and 70 through Ord.

According to "*Andreas' History of the State of Nebraska*" first published in 1882 by the The Western Historical Company, as part of the Kansas Collection, the town of Vinton was laid out in 1874 on land donated by the Burlington & Missouri River Railroad Company. General E.O.C. Ord, in command of the military along the Platte, had made a trip up the North Loup Valley to select a site for a fort, so the new town was named "Ord," in his honor. The only other place in the United States with this name is Fort Ord, California, named for the same man.

A military establishment was needed in the area that became Valley County because of fear of Indian attacks. Construction began on Fort Hartsuff in 1874, the year that grasshoppers had eaten all the crops. Building the compound was a Godsend, as the settlers were eager to find work, so they could buy food and supplies to survive the winter. The fort served the area until 1881 when the problem with Indians had subsided, and much of the land had been homesteaded. Dr.Glen Auble, interested in historic preservation, purchased the abandoned fort and in 1961, donated it to the State of Nebraska. It has now been restored with appropriate 1870s furnishings. As a state park it is open to the public and has a beautiful picnic area.

Last Stop: Ord, Valley County, Nebraska. Ord was named Valley County seat by its first 100 settlers. Within the first year a post office was established, a schoolhouse built, and the first courthouse was erected. Ord soon had all the necessary businesses to take care of the needs of the fledgling community. Water provided by the year-round flow of the North Loup River was an added benefit.

In 1880 about 35 structures were built, over half of them business houses. By the end of the year the population had increased to 250. In 1881 the entire town was threatened by a devastating fire, and the following year a defective flue caused another serious fire on the south side of the public square. Before it could be stopped, several more buildings were destroyed.

In 1882 the "*Ord Quiz*" newspaper was established. At least half a dozen McNamee's are memorialized through obituaries posted in the Ord Quiz.

By 1888 Ord had two railroad lines -- the Burlington and the Union Pacific -- transporting both freight and passengers. Barley, rye, and potatoes were sold locally and shipped out. Corn was raised for feeding livestock -- sheep, cattle, and hogs. The year 1888 also saw the establishment of the Ord Volunteer Fire Department.

Having painted the backdrop, let's explore the characters and place them in their proper places.

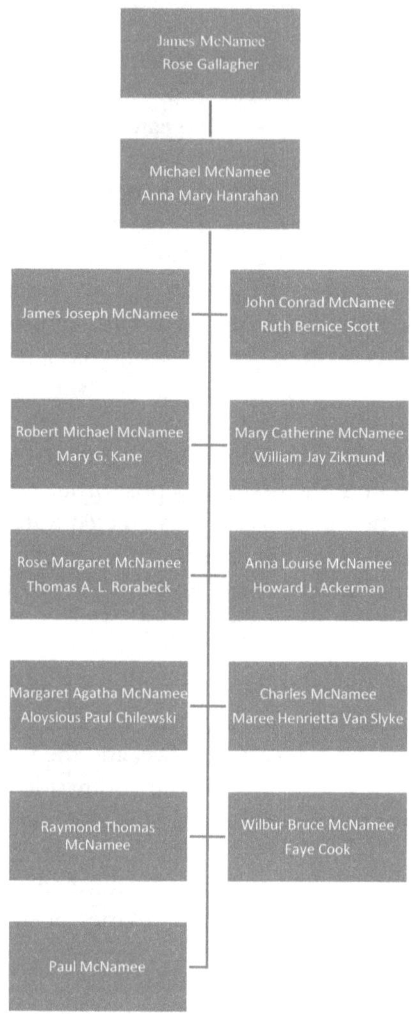

James McNamee
Rose Gallagher
Michael McNamee
Anna Mary Hanrahan
James Joseph McNamee
John Conrad McNamee
Ruth Bernice Scott
Robert Michael McNamee
Mary G. Kane
Mary Catherine McNamee
William Jay Zikmund
Rose Margaret McNamee
Thomas A. L. Rorabeck
Anna Louise McNamee
Howard J. Ackerman
Margaret Agatha McNamee
Aloysious Paul Chilewski
Charles McNamee
Maree Henrietta Van Slyke
Raymond Thomas McNamee
Wilbur Bruce McNamee
Faye Cook
Paul McNamee

5 JAMES MCNAMEE

James McNamee, the patriarch of the McNamee family, remains something of a mystery. A note on yellow legal paper handed down from Rose (McNamee) Rorabeck, who lived in Midwest, Wyoming in 1980 said only that *"Michael McNamee, born in Belfast, Ireland, came to [the] United States at age twelve with his parents and other members of their family."* Michael's parents were never named and remained a source of mystery until 2017 when I received Michael's death certificate in response to a request made to the Wyoming State Archives. There someone had recorded Michael's father…James.

There is the problem of missing relatives. The information given to me simply states that, *"Michael came to America at age 12 with his parents and other members of the family."* Further, the information said, *"He had a brother John and two sisters (Mollie and Mattie). One of the sisters married a McCarthy, the other married a McCartney."* One further clue came from Michael McNamee's obituary: The first stop mentioned on the McNamee journey was Lexington, Kentucky. What follows is the information uncovered that most closely fits the family lore given to me. I account for James, Michael, John, Mattie, and Mollie. I add a likely wife for James – Rose (Rosa) Gallagher (McNamee). For this portion of the book, I consulted with a professional genealogist who confirmed my research as the most likely scenario for the McNamee family. However! It is not definitive.

A likely candidate for patriarch James appears first in the 1880 U.S. Census for Kentucky. He was working a farm in Nicholasville, Kentucky. Modern day Nicholasville is a suburb of Lexington, Kentucky. He listed his age as 50 years old which would have put his birthday around 1830. His wife's name was Rosa (possibly Rose) and she also listed her age as 50. Both James and Rosa claimed Ireland as their birthplace. Living at home and earning his living as a baker, young Michael McNamee was 21 years old. The Census documents a sister Bettie (18 years old), a brother George who was 16 years old and worked as a farm hand, and a little sister Mary who was 13 years old and attending school. Michael and Bettie's birthplaces were listed as Ireland, while George and Mary's birthplaces were listed as Kentucky. This information is consistent with what we know about Michael and family. George, being born in the U.S. may never have moved West and therefore was lost to family memory.

Why is this likely the patriarch of the McNamee family? In all the coming-and-goings of the McNamee family documented in the *Ord Quiz*, there was never a mention of anyone ever visiting James or his wife. Nor does a matching James McNamee show up in any of the Nebraska or Missouri Census records. One likely explanation is that James never traveled West with his son. If indeed, James was about 50 years old in 1880 and having had young children to care for, perhaps he chose to stay in Kentucky. Certainly, son Michael was the right age to have traveled to Missouri where he met and married Anna Mary Hanrahan in 1891.

There is a record of Mrs. Rosa McNamee (age 68) dying of stomach cancer on December 28, 1895. She is buried at the Catholic Cemetery in Lexington, Kentucky. There is a record of James McNamee dying of organic heart failure on July 21, 1908. He was 72 years and 3 months old at the time which would have put his birthday approximately April 1836. He lived in Somerset, Fayette County, KY and is buried at the Catholic Cemetery in Lexington.

John McNamee - A likely match was found for another son, John McNamee. A Kentucky death certificate lists a John McNamee, a quarryman, who died on January 27, 1924 of "injuries sustained by being run down by a railroad train." John was 58 years old at the time which would have placed his birthday in 1866 – about the right time to be the John mentioned in the family history. Further, his death certificate lists his parents, James McNamee and Rose Gallagher, as being from Ireland. John does not show up in the 1880 Census as living with the McNamee family. However, his age in 1880 would have been about 14 years old. It was common in those days for a son to be apprenticed and living elsewhere. Tying this together, the death certificate information was provided by Charles E. McCarthy, a likely candidate for being the husband of Elizabeth "Bettie" McNamee, one of James's daughters born in Ireland.

Elizabeth "Bettie" McNamee – Bettie McNamee is not specifically mentioned in the family history handed down to me. However, the 1880 Census lists Bettie as one of James's Irish-born children. In 1880 she was 18 years old, which would have made her birthday in circa 1862. Bettie married Charles McCarthy in 1884. Thus, Bettie may be one of the two girls mentioned in the family history who married a McCarthy.

Martha "Mattie" McNamee – Mattie is a common nickname for Martha, Madeline, or Matilda. I uncovered a record of a Martha McCarthy, wife of Michael S. McCarthy (the person who provided the death details for John McNamee). It is possible that Martha is also one of the girls mentioned in the family lore. It is easy enough to conflate McCarthy and McCartney.

Mary "Mollie" McNamee – Mollie is a common nickname for

Mary or Margaret. The 1880 Census states James McNamee's youngest daughter was born in approximately 1867 in Kentucky. However, it was common on censuses to put a birth down as being from the same county in which the person resided rather than list the actual birthplace. This makes Mary McNamee a candidate for being the "Mollie" that came from Ireland with James and Michael.

6 MICHAEL MCNAMEE

(L-R) Thomas A. L. Rorabeck, Ruth Catherine Rorabeck, Rose Margaret (McNamee) Rorabeck, (Baby) Raymond Thomas Rorabeck, Anna Maree (Hanrahan) McNamee, Mary (Maloney) Rorabeck, Michael McNamee

How is it that so often we only find out in death who someone was in life? An obituary published in the *Ord Quiz* on September 19, 1935 gives us our first clear glimpse of Michael McNamee:

Michael McNamee was born in Belfast, Ireland, on May 22, 1854 and at the age of 12 came to America with his parents, locating at Lexington, Kentucky, later moving to Richmond, Missouri, where on August 8, 1890 [this date is incorrect] he was married to Anna May [Mary] Hanrahan. In February 1907, the family came to Valley county which has been the family home ever since.

According to family lore, Michael McNamee was the twin brother of James McNamee, both of whom were born in Belfast, Ireland in May, 1854. Twin brother James may or may not have been on the trip as he is said to have perished in infancy. As previously noted, Michael had a brother John and two sisters nicknamed Mollie and Mattie. It is not known what their given names were.

Michael's birthday is approximate. In the U.S. Census reports of 1900 - 1930, which normally gets its information directly from individuals,

Michael's birth month is May, but his birth year fell between 1854 and 1866. His death certificate lists his birthday as May 22, 1854. Michael's birthplace is also approximate. Although both his death certificate and his obituary state that Michael was born in Belfast, Ireland, no documented confirmation of this has been located. What is certain is that Michael himself stated on at least one Census survey that he had been born in Northern Ireland (which includes Belfast) and that Anna had been born in the Irish Free State.

Michael immigrated to America sometime between 1862 – 1876. There are many conflicts in the information sources on this. The most likely date is 1866. He was naturalized as a U.S. Citizen in 1883.

Michael first appears as a 21-year-old living on a farm in with his father James McNamee in Nicholasville, Kentucky in 1880. Michael worked as a baker.

As Michael McNamee made his way west, why he chose Missouri is not clear. It's possible that he was aware that another branch of the McNamee clan lived in Missouri at that time and the area near Franklin, Missouri was known as Little Ireland. It's also possible that he was lured west by the stories he would have read in the newspapers about the rich farmlands and opportunities available in Missouri.

Orrick, MO City Hall 2019

Between 1880 - 1891, Michael McNamee moved to Ray County, Missouri. He lived in the vicinity of Orrick. Orrick, laid out 1869, consisted of rich river bottom land and even today is one of the State's leading potato producing areas. Michael met and married Anna Marie Hanrahan in Richmond, Ray, Missouri in August 1, 1891 and lived there for about a decade before moving further West. All of their children were born in Missouri.

About 1907, the McNamee's moved from Missouri to Nebraska. The 1910 U.S. Census shows Michael and Anna Marie living in Vinton Valley, Nebraska.

Michael died at age 81 on September 12, 1935 of prostate cancer. He had traveled from his home in Valley County, Nebraska to visit the families of his two daughters, Rose Margaret (McNamee) Rorabeck and Anna Louise (McNamee) Ackerman, who lived in Midwest, Wyoming. Suffering from an onset of uremia, Michael was admitted to the Midwest Hospital on September 10th where he was attended to by a Dr. Haywood. After he passed away, Michael's family brought him home to Ord where funeral services were held at the Sowl Chapel. Reverend Charles F. Wantz, a popular preacher from Midvale United Brethren Church, presided at the last rites. According to a newspaper account,

"Mrs. Mark Tolen, accompanied at the piano by Mrs. Kirby McGrew, sang three beautiful solos. Pall bearers included R. C. Burrows, W. S. King, Oscar Travis, H. B. Thompson, Ed Verstraete and Frank Travis and the body was laid to rest in Ord Cemetery." (Ord Quiz, Sept. 19, 1935)

Anna Maree Hanrahan. Anna Maree (also, Mary or Marie) Hanrahan, was born in Lewis County, West Virginia in 1873. There was about a 14-year age difference between Michael and Anna Marie. Anna Marie's family was also originally from Kilkenny, Ireland. Altogether Michael and Anna Marie produced quite a pack of children. Eleven of them: John, James, Mary, Rose, Mike, Anna, Martha, Raymond, Wilbur, Paul, and Charles.

Perhaps this tribute from the *Ord Quiz* of June 1, 1933 best illustrates Anna Marie (Hanrahan) McNamee's life:

MRS. M. MCNAMEE TO HER REWARD

— Wife of well-known farmer dies Sunday after ten weeks of serious illness —
After an illness of ten weeks, Mrs. Michael McNamee passed away Sunday, May 28, 1933, in the Ord home of her daughter, Mrs. W. J. Zikmund, where she had been tenderly cared for during much of her long illness. Funeral services were held at Sowl's chapel Tuesday and interment was in the Ord Cemetery.

Anna, daughter of Thomas and Mary Hanrahan, was born Feb. 13, 1873 in Lewis County, West Virginia and at an early age went with her parents to Richmond, Mo. where her girlhood was spent and where she was married on August 1, 1891 to Michael McNamee. They lived in and near Richmond until February 1908 and then came to Valley County where the remainder of Mrs. McNamee's life was spent.

Seven sons and four daughters were born to Mrs. McNamee and all of them, as well as her husband, were at her bedside Sunday when death came. Her children are: James, John and Robert, of Ericson, Mrs. Catherine Zikmund and Mrs. Martha Chilewski, of Ord, Mrs. Rose Rorabeck and Mrs. Anna Ackerman, of Midwest, Wyo., Charles, Wilbur, Raymond and Paul, all of whom live in Ord. One sister, Mrs. Margaret Rorabeck, of Lavina, Mont., was also at her bedside. She is also survived by two brothers: John Hanrahan, Los Angeles, CA, and James Hanrahan of Centerville, Iowa and will be mourned by twelve grandchildren.

A devoted wife and mother who always thought first of her family, Mrs. McNamee will be sadly missed. Although unable to attend church regularly, she was a true Christian whose many good deeds and kindly acts will be long remembered.

Life in Ord, Nebraska

Anna Maree McNamee with four of her sons. Charles McNamee is third from left. others are unidentified. Photo undated.

Michael and Anna Mary seem to have nurtured a strong family bond. For many years the local newspaper, the *Ord Quiz* carried stories of the comings-and-goings of the eleven children as they grew up and created families of their own. McNamee boys were noted doing chores for the neighbors. McNamee girls won ribbons for their cooking at the county fair. What follows are excerpts of stories gleaned from the paper that give some insight to the life of the McNamee family in Nebraska.

Ord Quiz - April 28, 1910. Last Thursday the suit of T. J. Nethery against Mike McNamee, a tenant on the Nethery farm (of Ord) was tried before Judge Godmundsen and to a jury. Mr. Nethery thought he did not get his share of the rent last year, but the jury thought otherwise, finding for the defendant (Mike McNamee). $18 was the amount in question.

Although the U.S. Census survey of 1920 indicates that the McNamee's lived on a rented farm, a newspaper announcement about an equipment and livestock sale stated that Michael had purchased a farm around 1919.

On November 20, 1919, William Reeves and Mike McNamee announced they planned to hold a combination sale on the old Steve Brace farm Southwest of Ord on December 5, 1919. Mr. Reeves planned to return to Kansas and wanted to sell all his personal property. Mr. McNamee had recently bought a farm and had more stock and machinery than he had immediate use for. They stated that this would be a "big sale, with lots of horses, cattle, machinery and grain."

The Reeves-McNamee Sale

Mr. Reeves has decided to return to Kansas and will make a cleanup of all of his personal property, and Mr. McNamee has bought a farm and finds that he has more machinery and stock than he wants so will reduce his holdings in this way. They will sell the following described property at the old Brace place 5 1-2 miles southwest of Ord and 1 1-2 miles north of Vinton on

FRIDAY, DEC. 5

Eleven Horses

Black mare 9 years old, wt. 1500.
Brown mare 9 years old, wt. 1400.
Brown horse 6 years old, wt. 1500.
Bay mare smooth mouth, wt. 1400.
Gray horse smooth mouth, wt. 1400.
Span bay geldings 2 years old, wt. 2100.
Gray gelding 2 years old, wt. 1050.
Two brown mare yearling colts.
Gelding colt 1 year old.

58 Head of Cattle

Three head of good milch cows all giving milk and all young cows.
Twelve head of good milch cows, two with calves by side, three of them Holsteins.
Fourteen spring calves. Five yearling heifers. Five yearling steers.
Hereford bull 3 years old, a good one.
Twenty-eight head of good stock cows.

Twenty Head of Spring Shoats, weight about 125 pounds each

Machinery

Deering grain binder; McCormick mower; John Deere hay rake, new; John Deere side hitch hay sweep, new; Emerson 2-row lister, new; single row lister; 14-inch Cassady gang plow, new; Emerson 2-row; single row John Deere; Bayler 2-row cultivator, new; single row cultivator; Emerson 8-foot cut disc, new; 2-section harrow; Emerson stalk drill, new; Peoria grain drill with grass seed attachment; 16-inch walking plow; Newton wagon with top box, new; low wagon and box; hay rack; new grind stone; two sets of harness and fly nets; McCormick binder nearly new; Case sulkey plow 16-inch; two John Deere lister corn cultivators, 2-row; Badger cultivator; John Deere cultivator; John Deere disc; P. and O. lister; St. Jor lister; set steel wagon wheels for truck; 10-foot McCormick hay rake; 8-foot rake; Moline cultivator.

Grain and Hay

Two stacks of alfalfa, about 1800 bushels of ear corn and a few oats.

Household Goods

South Bend malleable range, new; heating stove; kitchen cabinet, new; dining room table and twelve chairs; three rockers; dresser and three beds; Axminister rug 8 1-2 x 10 1-2; organ; book case; sewing machine; Old Trusty incubator, 150-egg size; washing machine and wringer; separator; some potatoes and fruit.

BIG FREE LUNCH AT 11:30, SALE TO FOLLOW AT ONCE

TERMS—Sums of $10 and under cash, sums over that amount 8 months time will be given on bankable paper at 10 per cent interest. No property to be removed from the place until settled for.

Wm. Reeves and Mike McNamee, Props.

RAY BURDICK and
ERNEST WELLER, Auctioneers.   FIRST NATIONAL BANK, Clerk

The McNamee's showed off their farming skills at the North Loup Valley Fair in September 1920. Mike McNamee, Jr. won prizes for his boars and sow pigs including Mortensen's "special best young boar," "special best sow," and Milford's special. Anna Mary McNamee was awarded several prizes for her very pumpkins, summer squash, parsnips, black-eyed peas, Indian sweet corn, Red Kidney beans, winter onions and lettuce. The Fair came just in time. The first frost of the season had already burned some crops and there was general worry that everything would be lost before the Fair could be held. But the weather stayed mild and everything turned out just fine.

In other news that month, the Ord firemen were able to successfully get out the vote in support of a $55,000 bond issue to build a new city hall and home for the firemen. When news of their success got out "the enthusiasm of the boys and their friends over-flowed and they started a demonstration that lasted until midnight and ended in a big feed at Brady's restaurant with the Mayor and most of the councilmen present helping to put on the program." Two months later, Warren G. Harding was elected President leading a Republican sweep of the elections and ending up with Republican control of the House and Senate. Nebraska overwhelmingly voted Republican as well.

March 1924 - Spring had come to Vinton Valley, Nebraska with a vengeance. Heavy rains made many roads nearly impassable. Wencel Bruha, whose was always so proud of his Ford automobile, ended up calling it quits after the "awful roads" broke the driveshaft on his car and he had to put his saddle horse to work "which he should have done in the first place." Over in

Barker, people had just about given up hope of having nice weather so that Spring planting could begin, and school attendance had dropped considerably "on account of the weather, sickness and several other things." Ezra Miska in Haskell Creek noted that there was nothing much to write about but mud. "There sure is lots of it and keeps everyone from going about more than is necessary."

But people were optimistic. Frank Dworak's store was offering "New Stock of Groceries and Queensware! We deliver! Just dial 83 on your telephone." Farmer's Grain and Supply Company was "Ready with a Spring line of Merchandise that is extremely attractive in quality and price." House dresses were a $1.15 each; gauze vests with wing sleeves "something you have wanted for a long while" were priced at 60 cents to $1.25 a suit. The Ord Theater featured "The Sunshine Trail" a western comedy featuring actor Douglas McLean. Admission was 10 cents and 25 cents. Ironically, the hot topic of the day in the news was a vitriolic debate as to whether theaters should be allowed to show movies on Sunday.

In New Yale, the McNamee's did not let the weather slow them down. Mike McNamee was busy hauling oats for Zack Greenwalt. Charley McNamee hauled a load of lumber for Frank Lumney. Louie Greenwalt hauled hay for Bob McNamee. When work was done, the McNamee's, Mike, Anna, and son Charley paid a visit to the Greenwalt's for an evening of cards.

The McNamee family were close friends with the Van Slyke family. On February 24, 1927, Henry Clayton Van Slyke got out of the farming business. He did so reluctantly. As he would tell anyone who would listen, he was forced to quit because the farm he rented 5 miles East of Ord was sold out from under him and he could not find a suitable new place to rent. So, on March 2, 1927, Weller & McMindes Auction Company conducted a clean-up sale of Henry's entire farm. The Van Slyke's moved to Olean Township following the sale.

Arthur Van Slyke got some good news in January 1930. He had been home in Olean Township since before the Christmas holidays when he found out that he had been hired as the new driver on the morning bus. There is a photo of a proud Charles McNamee and Art Van Slyke showing off in their snappy bus driver uniforms. Both young men were employed by the Cornhusker Bus Lines and were "stationed" in Hastings, Nebraska. Later, Charles would move to the Cornhusker Depot in Cheyenne, Wyoming.

Arthur Van Slyke and Charles McNamee

NEW YALE NEWS – March 3, 1927 - Mike McNamee called on Jim Wozniak Sunday. Andy Phlaster helped Mike McNamee haul corn a few days this week. Ernest Jensen called on Mike McNamee Sunday. Mrs. Louis Chilewski spent the week with her folks Mr. and Mrs. Mike McNamee. Sunday visitors at Mike McNamee's were Mr. and Mrs. Wm. Zigmund of Ord. Mr. and Mrs. Louis Chelewski and Bob McNamee. Ed Nelson shelled corn for Mike McNamee Monday.

Ord Quiz – March 8, 1927 - COUNTY BOARD PROCEEDINGS – On account of error in time previously turned in and allowed, and upon advice from Mr. Juergens that they are entitled to same for labor on highway, it was moved and seconded that Hunter Jones, Loyal Ford, Robert McNamee, and Edward Lee be paid for their labor. Robert received $42.00.

Ord Quiz – February 19, 1931 - SPRING CREEK NEWS – Friday (Feb 13) was Mrs. Mike (Anna Maree) McNamee's birthday and she and Mr. McNamee took supper with Will Zikmund's. When they returned home, they discovered their sons and neighbors had made up a surprise party for her. The evening was spent like most parties are and at a late hour refreshments were served.

Ord Quiz – March 19, 1931 - James McNamee and Tom Hanrahan were at Mike McNamee's Sunday. Three days later on March 22, 1931, Mrs. Mike McNamee and Wilbur and Charley McNamee and family (Maree,

Bobby, Charlotte) went to Lincoln Monday, returning Tuesday. Charley returned to his home at Grand Island Wednesday.

Ord Quiz – July 30, 1931 - Friends and neighbors gathered at Mike McNamee's Saturday evening and gave a surprise party for Mrs. (Anna Maree) McNamee, who is leaving this Wednesday for a trip to Wyoming and Montana.

Mrs. Chas (Maree Henrietta) McNamee and children came from Grand Island to visit the Van Slyke home. She returned to Grand Island accompanied by her mother, Mrs. Van Slyke.

Mr. and Mrs. Wilbur McNamee stayed at the Cook farm doing chores while the Cook family left on an auto trip to Ohio.

7 JAMES JOSEPH MCNAMEE

The first of the 11 children born to Michael and Anna Mary McNamee was born in Richmond, Missouri on Christmas Eve, December 24, 1891 barely five months after his parents were married. His father, Michael, was 37 and his mother, Anna, was 18. The *Chillicothe Constitution-Tribune*, the closest newspaper serving the Richmond area, did not record a birth announcement but did note that Christmas was a mess of icy roads and heavy snow.

James spent his childhood helping out on the family's rented farm in Richmond, Ray County, Missouri; moving with his family to Vinton Valley, Nebraska at age 19 in 1910. Sometime in the next 7 years, James left home but didn't go very far. He rented a farm in the same town as his father and paid regular visits to his parents on weekends and for family holiday celebrations.

Between 1917 and 1918 approximately 24 million men completed a World War I draft registration. The McNamee brothers, like millions of others, went down to their local draft board in Valley County and signed up. When he registered for the draft in WWI (June 5, 1917 at age 25), James was single and described as Short, Medium build with Gray eyes and Dark Brown hair. He listed his occupation as a self-employed farmer. He registered with his brother John Conrad McNamee (age 22). Later that same year (Sept. 12), younger brother Michael McNamee (age 18) also signed up for the draft.

James never married. He does appear to have been close friends with Thomas Hanrahan, the nephew-in-law of his mother Anna Mary. Thomas was about the same age as James. Thomas lived, for at least some time, in the household of his uncle-in-law, Michael McNamee. Later local newspaper accounts of comings-and-goings around Ord, Nebraska noted that James and Thomas often showed up at Michael's home for dinner and other social events.

In April 1930, James lived with his sister Mary Catherine (McNamee) Zikmund and her husband William J. Zikmund at their home at 100 R Street, Ord, Nebraska. Thirty-four years old at the time, James worked as a filling station attendant.

In 1932, James was the subject of a lawsuit that went all the way to the Nebraska Supreme Court. It seems that James had enrolled as a student in the Ord Linotype Business School. Like modern college students, James took out a tuition loan in the form of a promissory note to Irl D. Tolen, who then ran the linotype school. The note was in the amount of $1,100. Unknown to James, Mr. Tolen then used the promissory note, along with other promissory notes, as collateral for linotype machines he purchased from Mergenthaler Linotype Company. When the Mergenthaler Company demanded that James pay off the loan, James refused, saying he had not been notified that his note had been passed along to someone else and that he was not obligated to the Mergenthaler Company. The District Court sided with James on the grounds that Tolen had a legal obligation to give a copy of the note to James and notify him that the debt was then owned by another company. Mergenthaler appealed the ruling to the Nebraska Supreme Court. The court heard the case on April 6, 1933. Attorney John P. Misko was there looking after James McNamee's interests and Attorny C. M. Davis was representing the linotype company. On June 29, 1933, the newspaper reported, "John P. Misko, of the law firm of Hardenbrook & Misko, last week won the first case that he has argued before the Nebraska Supreme Court when the court found for James McNamee in the case of Mergenthaler Linotype Company v. McNamee."

Between 1930 – 1935, James moved again to take up residence as a lodger in the home of Anthony and Nettie Thills of 2011 K Street, Ord, Nebraska. Mr. Thills owned his own home and his own mechanic shop and employed James who listed himself as a garage mechanic. He lived at this address until at least April 1940.

REGISTRATION CARD—(Men born on or after April 28, 1877 and on or before February 16, 1897)

SERIAL NUMBER — U. 493

1. Name (Print): James Joseph McNamee

ORDER NUMBER

2. Place of Residence (Print): Gen Ord Valley Nebr.

[THE PLACE OF RESIDENCE GIVEN ON THE LINE ABOVE WILL DETERMINE LOCAL BOARD JURISDICTION; LINE 2 OF REGISTRATION CERTIFICATE WILL BE IDENTICAL]

3. Mailing Address: Gen Del Ord. Nebr.

4. Telephone —

5. Age in Years: 50

Date of Birth: 24 1871

6. Place of Birth: Richmond Missouri

7. Name and Address of Person Who Will Always Know Your Address: Mrs. William J Zickmund, Ord Nebr.

8. Employer's Name and Address: Anderson Motor Co Ord Nebr

9. Place of Employment or Business: Ord Valley Nebr.

I Affirm That I Have Verified Above Answers And That They Are True.

Jas. J. McNamee.

D. S. S. Form 1 (Revised 4-1-42)

REGISTRAR'S REPORT

DESCRIPTION OF REGISTRANT

RACE		HEIGHT (Approx.)	WEIGHT (Approx.)	COMPLEXION	
White	X	5-3"	135	Sallow	
		EYES	HAIR	Light	
Negro		Blue ✓	Blonde	Ruddy	V
		Gray	Red	Dark	
Oriental		Hazel	Brown X	Freckled	
		Brown	Black	Light brown	
Indian		Black	Gray ✓	Dark brown	
			Bald	Black	
Filipino					

Other obvious physical characteristics that will aid in identification.

(NONE)

I certify that my answers are true, that the person registered has read or has had read to him his own answers, that I have witnessed his signature or mark and that all of his answers of which I have knowledge are true, except as follows:

Geo. H. Allen
Signature of registrant

Registrar for Local Board _Ord_
(County)   (City or county)   (State)

Date of registration _4-27-42_

Local Board No. 1   76
Valley County   175

001

Nebr. State Bank Bldg.

(The stamp of the Local Board having jurisdiction of the registrant shall be placed in the above space)

The Fourth Registration for the World War II selective service was often called the "Old Man's Draft," because it registered men who were 45 to 64 years old at the time. When James, by then age 50, signed up for the draft again in WW II (March 27, 1942), his height was listed as 5'3", weight as 135 lbs, and hair as Brown and Gray. His eyes were Blue, and his complexion was "ruddy." He was employed by the Anderson Motor Company (an auto and farm equipment dealer) of Ord, Neb. As in the first World War, brother John Conrad (age 48) also went with him to sign up for the draft. John was employed by the City Street Dept. of Beatrice, Nebraska.

James died at the age of 51 on January 2, 1944 at the Grand Island hospital. According to a short obituary in the *Ord Quiz*, James was taken suddenly ill with pneumonia in early January. He had been employed by a Grand Island, Nebraska laundry service. His death was sudden and unexpected. Funeral services were held at the Hastings-Zikmund Chapel in Ord with Reverend M. M. Long officiating.

At the time of James's death his brother John lived in Beatrice,

Nebraska. Charles and Raymond lived in Cheyenne, Wyoming. Robert Michael lived in Valentine. Wilber of Groveport, O. Paul in Ord. His sisters, Mrs. W. J. Zikmund lived in Ord. Mrs Thomas Rorabeck lived in Midwest, Wyo. Mrs. H. D. Ackerman lived in Casper, Wyo and Mrs. Louie Chilewski lived in Comstock. He was buried in the Ord cemetery.

8 JOHN CONRAD MCNAMEE

The second child born to Michael and Anna Mary McNamee, John (Jack) Conrad McNamee was also born in Richmond, Ray County, Missouri on March 2, 1894.

As a side note, the first formal education in Ray County, Missouri began in 1819 as a subscription school. In modern terms this would be a charter school. As the population increased, other subscription schools were established. According to the Richmond High School website, the first public school was a two-room brick structure constructed on East North Main Street in 1859. Sometime after that, the Presbyterian Church established what would become Richmond College (which taught high school courses in its building). The Christian Church established an "academy" essentially an elementary and middle school. It is also interesting to note that in the late 1890s and early 1900s, there were over 90 schools in Ray County. At least seven of the McNamee children attended classes in these schools.

Like his older brother and all the McNamee siblings, John probably had farm chores to take care of. Two newspapers, the *Missouri and Arkansas Farmer and Fruitman* and the *Missouri and Kansas Farmer*, promoted the settlement of southwest Missouri, southeast Kansas, and northwest Arkansas. Established in the 1880s, these newspapers printed testimonials from settlers and visitors about the area's rich agricultural promise. Author Laura Ingalls Wilder in her book *On The Way Home* wrote of arriving in Mansfield, Missouri in 1894 by wagon having traveled from South Dakota and of facing "danger and fear, full of unfamiliar faces, unpredictable roads, and inclement weather." Photos of farming life published by the State Horticultural Society of Missouri in 1894 depict a hard life for the farming industry.

Still single when he registered for the draft in World War 1 on June 5, 1917, 23-year-old John was of Medium height, Medium build, with Gray eyes and Dark Brown hair. Like his brother James, he was a self-employed farmer. But in truth, he lived on the farm with his Dad Michael and his brothers and sisters. We got more detail when he registered for the World War II draft (April 27, 1942). His height was 5'6" and weight was 145. Eyes were blue and hair brown.

Marriage came late for John. On September 10, 1930 John married the widow Ruth Bernice Scott of Plum Creek, Pawnee, Nebraska. Ruth, known to most of the family by her middle name, Bernice, the daughter of

Thomas Chalmers Scott and Lorena Jones, had been married before. In 1926 at the age of 15 she married David Hurtie (or Hustie) and produced a son, Wayne David, born about 1927. As a side note, several newspaper articles noted that Wayne served with the U.S. Marines in China. It's not clear how David Hurtie died. Born December 13, 1910, Ruth Bernice Scott was 19 when she married 36-year-old John. By all accounts, Jack well and truly loved Bernice.

The couple moved to Beatrice in 1937. The couple was active in their Presbyterian church. Bernice appeared in several newspaper articles as an active member of the Presbyterian Women's Service Society. At one point in 1943, Bernice had a grand time with her lady friends as part of The Jolly Neighbors Club. John, too, appears in several instances as involved in church leadership. Things appeared to be going well for them.

John is listed in 1942 as working for the City Street Department. He stayed busy at this for quite a while. In June 1944 John and a Mr. H. R. Everett were busy grading roads in Island Grove Township, a small town a few miles southeast of Beatrice. John (Jack) and brother Charles McNamee went briefly into the road construction business around 1944-45 in Beatrice, Nebraska. But the business ultimately had to close after Charles got ill and had to return to Cheyenne, Wyoming. According to John's obituary, he worked for the Board of Public Works until his retirement in 1966.

The August 18, 1946 edition of the Beatrice Daily Sun carried the tragic news that Janice June McNamee, the two-year-old daughter of John and Bernice, died after drinking some gasoline. Janice June was born June 23, 1944 in Beatrice. The accident cast a deep shadow over the marriage.

On March 10, 1950, Ruth (Bernice) filed for divorce from John. In court filings she charged John "with being ill-tempered and abusive in action and speech and had struck her." She obtained a restraining order against him. The judge found in her favor and gave her custody of the children and ordered John to pay $65 a month in child support. A few months later, in an unusual move, John retaliated by filing a countersuit in district court and requested a new trial based on his assertion that Bernice was the one at fault "and the cause of breaking up of this home." He claimed, "that the award of $65 per month was arbitrary and unreasonable." The case went to the Nebraska Supreme Court and in April 1951, the State Supreme Court upheld the District Court's ruling and granted John the divorce from Ruth but modified the divorce settlement. The court gave custody of one minor child (which one is not clear) to John and the other to Ruth. They awarded Ruth $750 as proceeds of the sale of some property the couple owned with the balance going to John. The court also awarded $150 to Ruth to cover attorney fees.

John died on April 22, 1968 in Beatrice, Gage, Nebraska. He was 74 years old. Fox DeBuhr Funeral Home took care of John's arrangements. He is buried at Evergreen Home Cemetery.

Ruth Bernice McNamee lived to be 80 years old. She died on Friday, May 17, 1991 at the Beatrice Community Hospital. She worked for the Beatrice State Developmental Center as a cook for 28 years before retiring in 1976. She is also buried at Evergreen.

9 ROBERT MICHAEL MCNAMEE

The third child of Michael and Anna McNamee, Robert was born in Richmond, Missouri on March 21, 1895. He lived with the family until about 1930.

On September 12, 1918, he registered for the draft in World War I. Listed his age as 18 (he was actually 23) and his birthday as 21 March 1900. At the time, he worked as a farmer for his father, Michael McNamee. He is described as being of medium height, medium build, with blue eyes and brown hair.

On December 19, 1929 he married 15-year-old Mary G. Kane of Burchard, a small village in Pawnee County, Nebraska. They were blessed with their only child, a son named Robert William McNamee, on November 22, 1930. Mary was born in Burchard, Nebraska on June 9, 1914 to Martin and Maude (Mooney) Kane. Mary, lived in various towns in Nebraska; moved to Kearney, attended Nursing School and graduated from the Vocational School of Practical Nursing in Kearney, Nebraska in 1963. Mary worked with Drs. Wilcox, Richardson and Jester; was later a nurse and then charge nurse at Mount Carmel Home until she retired. Mary, and presumably Robert, was a member of St. James Catholic Church, Kearney. Mary, age 90, died on June 14, 2004 in Omaha, Nebraska and is buried at the Kearney Cemetery.

Between 1935 – 1940 Robert and Mary bought a home at 210 Hall St. in Valentine City, Nebraska. Robert was a mechanic for the Nebraska Department of Roads and Irrigation at a salary of $1,320 a year. Their home was valued at $1,200. Wife Mary had left high school after her sophomore year.

By 1950, Robert had risen to become the Superintendent of the Central Nebraska Public Power and Irrigation District. The city directory showed them living a 1707 W. 6th Ave. in Hastings, Nebraska. Robert was considered "stand-offish" by the family.

Robert died of unknown causes on March 19, 1975 at the ripe age of 80 years old.

10 MARY CATHERINE MCNAMEE

The fourth child and first daughter of Michael and Anna (Hanrahan) McNamee, Mary Catherine McNamee was born in Richmond, Missouri on March 5, 1896. Along with the rest of the McNamee family, she moved to Valley County, Nebraska at age 11.

At age 27, Mary married William Jay Zikmund in Gering, Scotts Bluff, Nebraska on May 26, 1923. Their marriage produced four children: Two girls, Ardis A. and Vivian J. and two boys, Leroy and Lores L. The Zikmund family and the McNamee's were neighbors so Mary probably knew William all her life.

In 1930 the Zikmund family lived in a home they owned at 100 R. Street, Ord, Nebraska. The home was valued at $2,000. All four children, two boys and two girls lived at home. Mary Catherine's brother James Joseph also lived with them at the time. Husband William J. Zikmund made his living as a truck driver. Between 1930 and 1935, the Mary and family had bought another home at 2204 M. Street in Ord. William had taken up farming by 1940 and one of the daughters, Ardis was working as a stenographer at the County Assistance Office.

Sadly, husband William passed away on July 6, 1961. Mary Catherine lived another 8 years, passing away on May 30, 1969 at the Valley County Hospital after a short illness. Presbyterian Rites were held for her at the First Presbyterian Church in Ord, Nebraska. She was 73 years old. Rev. Kenneth Bunnell officiated at the 2:30 pm services on the Sunday following her death. Interment was in the Ord City Cemetery with Hastings-Pearson Mortuary in charge.

The Ord Quiz (June 5, 1969) noted: *She is survived by two sons, Leroy and Lores Lee, both of Ord; two daughters, Mrs. Vivian Williams of Ord and Mrs. Ardis McIntyre of Denver, Colo.; three brothers, Robert McNamee of Kearney, Wilbur McNamee of Groveport, Ohio, and Raymond McNamee of Eugene, Ore.; three sisters, Mrs. Anna Ackerman and Mrs. Rose Rorabeck, both of Casper, Wyo., and Mrs. Martha Chilewski of Comstock; plus three grandchildren. Her parents and four brothers also preceded her in death.*

11 ROSE MARGARET MCNAMEE

The fifth child and second daughter of Michael and Anna Mary (Hanrahan) McNamee, Rose Margaret McNamee was born in Richmond, Missouri on February 1, 1898. Rose's original name may have been Rosa. She is referred to by that name early on in the Census roles. Possibly she was named after her grandmother Rosa.

Rose lived on the McNamee family farm until about 1920. Sometime between 1920 and 1926, she had moved to Lavina, Montana where she worked as a clerk in the post office.

The September 23, 1926 edition of the *Ord Quiz* reported:

ROSE MCNAMEE WEDS; TO LIVE IN WYOMING

Miss Rose McNamee, daughter of Mr. and Mrs. Michael McNamee, was married on Sept. 5 (1926) to Thomas A. L. Rorabeck, son of Mr. and Mrs. M. Rorabeck, Rygate, Mont., at the home of Mr. and Mrs. R. E. Rorabeck at Lavina, Montana. Only a few relatives and close friends were present. The ceremony was performed by Rev. Alice Payne of the M. E. Church at six o'clock. After the ceremony a bountiful supper was served by Mrs. Rorabeck.

Those present were Mr. and Mrs. M. McNamee, Arcadia; Mr. and Mrs. M. Rorabeck and son Dave, Rygate, Mont., Mr. and Mrs. James Lockman, Rygate, Mont., Mr. and Mrs. Jens Harksen, Casper, Wyo., and Mr. and Mrs. R. E. Rorabeck.

Mrs. Rorabeck, nee McNamee, had been employed previous to her marriage in the post office and Lavina, Mont. The groom is employed at Midwest, Wyo., where the young couple will make their home.

In 1930, Thomas Rorabeck worked as a gas engine operator for a gasoline plant in Natrona County, Wyoming. They made their home on Gas Plant Road, south of Midwest, Wyoming and appeared to have stayed there for quite some time. In 1959, Thomas had become an engineer and Rose still lived at their home in Midwest. According to the City Directory of Casper, Wyoming, Midwest was:

"The center of the Salt Creek Oil Fields. This is the center of the Stanolind Oil & Gas Company oil fields and not an incorporated city. Located 45 miles north of Casper, the nearest banking point, its population approsimates 3,000."

Rose and Thomas were blessed with two children: Ruth Catherine and Raymond Thomas Rorabeck. Rosa passed away on January 10, 1987 in Natrona, Wyoming and is buried at Natrona Memorial Gardens in Casper, Wyoming.

12 ANNA LOUISE MCNAMEE

Anna Louise McNamee was child number six for Michael and Anna Mary McNamee. Born in Richmond, Missouri on February 28, 1902. When she was five years old, according to her obituary, the family moved to Ord, Nebraska.

On February 28, 1923, Anna Louise married Howard Darrell Ackerman of Iowa in Ord. Howard was born on October 6, 1900. They were blessed with at least three children: Mary Louise (1924), James H. (possibly Howard J.) (1930), and Martha Ann Greenland of Anchorage, Alaska. There may be another daughter, Phyllis. Howard's was a driver and a gas engine repair technician. When Howard registered for the draft in World War II, he was described as a "ruddy" man with blue eyes and brown hair. Standing about 5 feet, 11 inches tall, he weighed 190 pounds. Howard died, cause unknown, in Casper, Wyoming on March 16, 1953.

While Howard was alive, the family lived in a series of apartments in the Casper, Wyoming area. In 1930 they lived in the Consolidated Camp Precinct of Wyoming. Not sure if this was maybe related to the Great Depression. In 1939 they rented an apartment at 729 W. Railroad Ave. In 1945 they rented an apartment at 233 S. Jackson St. where Anna Louise was employed as the Manager of Traylor Apartments. In 1949 – 1952 they lived at 1140 W. 11th St. in Casper.

After a brief illness, she died at the Natrona County Memorial Hospital on March 1, 1979 and is buried in the Highland Cemetery of Casper, Wyoming.

13 MARTHA AGATHA MCNAMEE

Wilbur, Martha, Ray McNamee

Martha became the seventh child of Michael and Anna McNamee when she came into the world on January 6, 1905 in Richmond, Missouri. She married Aloysious Paul Chilewski on February 15, 1926 in Grand Island, Nebraska. Paul was a farmer but by 1940 was working as a garage manager in Comstock, Nebraska.

On February 18, 1926 the *Ord Quiz* proudly carried the following announcement: From the *Grand Island Independent* we glean the information that Miss Martha McNamee and Louie Chelewski (*sp*) both of this vicinity were issued a license to wed at Grand Island Monday and we assume that they were married the same day. Congratulations.

They were blessed with four children: Phyllis Mae (1929 – 1997), Charles Harold (1931 – 1997), Virginia (1936 - ?), and George Louis (1937 – 2011).

Martha passed away on December 2, 1983 in Comstock, Custer, Nebraska and is buried in the Ord Cemetery.

14 CHARLES MCNAMEE

Charles McNamee was born May 19, 1906 in Orrick, Missouri. By 1910, Michael and Anna Mary had moved the family to Ord, Nebraska. On June 1, 1927, at age 20, he married Marie Henrietta Van Slyke, a pretty 16-year-old girl who had been born on November 18, 1910 in Ord, Antelope County, Nebraska.

At the age of 23, Charles worked for Interstate Transit Lines as a driver. He paid $50 a month to rent their small home at 2109 1st Ave, Kearney City, Nebraska where they produced two children, Charlotte Maree and Bobby Deane. They moved to Cheyenne, Wyoming in about 1931 and rented a home at 2510 Evans Ave.

Though he traveled all over the country as a driver for the bus lines, Charles was devoted to Maree. In his wallet he carried a lock of Maree's fine brown hair for the rest of his life.

Unfortunately, Maree contracted tuberculosis. She died on September 13, 1934 in Basin, Big Horn County, Wyoming. Charles moved to Cheyenne later that year or early 1935. By 1940, the McNamee's had moved to 717 W. Pershing Boulevard, Cheyenne, Wyoming. Charles's salary as a bus driver was $2,250 and their home, which they owned was valued at $4,750.00.

Charles, in addition to driving for Interstate Transit Lines, may also have been an owner of the company. Interstate

Transit Lines eventually merged with Cornhusker Stage Lines. Charles retired from Cornhusker Stage Lines, receiving a watch commemorating 12 years of safe driving. Cornhusker Stage Lines eventually became part of the Greyhound Bus Lines.

Charles registered for the World War II draft on October 16, 1940. He listed his birthdate as May 19, 1907, which made him 33 years old. His listed his place of birth as Orrick, Missouri and his home address as 717 W. Pershing Blvd., Cheyenne, Laramie County, Wyoming. He listed Bernadine Elsa McNamee as his wife and next of kin and his employer as Union Pacific Stages of 2116 Leavenworth St. Omaha, Douglas County, Nebraska. He was not a tall man. His height was 5' 7", weight was 136 pounds, his complexion was light, his eyes were brown and his hair was black. He also had a scar on the back of his neck.

Charles died on May 25, 1946 in Memorial Hospital, Cheyenne, WY. Immediate cause of death was listed as Uremia due to chronic arteriosclerosis which in turn was due to "marked hypertension." He also suffered from pericarditis - Edema. He had been a patient at the hospital for 3 weeks prior to his death. He had lived in Cheyenne for 15 years (since 1931). His residence at the time of his death was listed as 801 W. 1st Ave, Cheyenne, WY. He lived there with second wife Bernadine Elsa McNamee. Charles is buried at the Bethel Cemetery

Maree Henrietta Van Slyke was born on November 18, 1910 in Ord, Antelope, Nebraska as the third child of Henry Clayton Van Slyke and Anna Maree Ludington. She had four siblings, namely, Floyd Leland, Arthur Conroy, Eva Nadyne, and Anna Evalene. Until she was married, Maree lived with her parents in Noble, Valley County, Nebraska.

The Henry Clayton Van Slyke family was prominent in Ord. Henry's daughter, Maree Henrietta Van Slyke, was a regular contributor to the *Ord Quiz* newspaper. As love blooms in the spring, perhaps it was that Maree began to take notice of Charlie McNamee in the spring of 1925. In her column, Maree wrote that *"Charlie McNamee ate dinner and spent the afternoon Sunday at Henry Van Slyke's"* after spending most of the week husking corn for Henry.

(L – R): Charles McNamee, Elvina (Thomsen) Van Slyke, Floyd Leland Van Slyke, Maree Henrietta Van Slyke, Anna Maree (Ludington) Van Slyke, Eva (Huebner) Van Slyke, Evaline (Day) Van Slyke, Henry Clayton Van Slyke

Maree Henrietta Van Slyke married Charles McNamee in Ord, Nebraska, on June 1, 1927. He was 21, she was 16 years old. A daughter, Charlotte Maree McNamee, was born on January 1, 1929 at her grandfather's farm in Ord, Nebraska.

According to the *Ord Quiz*, by December, 1929, Maree had not been home for a while and was probably not in the best of health. So she decided to go home for the holidays. The newspaper noted that Maree's "young daughter" had accompanied her to New Yale Township on Christmas Eve to visit her family. The next day, Maree's sister Eva Van Slyke drove with her back to Kearney.

In March 1930 Maree's parents and family drove to Kearney. Her mother, Anna Maree Ludington, decided to stay for an extended visit to help her daughter rest and "endeavoring to regain her strength" as "she had been sick all winter." Maree recovered enough by mid-April 1930 to return to Olean to visit her parents, bringing along "her small daughter" Charlotte Maree McNamee.

Husband Charles was able to break away from work in Hastings to come along during Maree's visit home in June 1930. The Universal News Reel at the air-conditioned Idyll Hour Theater (It's COOL inside!) in Greeley, Nebraska featured another, more famous, Graham McNamee at the microphone. The U. S.

Maree with Charlotte Maree McNamee

Census supervisor, H. G. Webbert, issued a press release announcing that the official population of Valley County in 1930 was 9,532 people living on 1,297 farms. But his figures were off by just a tiny bit.

It was a Sunday June 22, 1930 during this visit home that the McNamee's welcomed the newest member of the family. A 9-pound baby boy, Bobby Deane McNamee, was born at the Henry Clayton Van Slyke home. Charles went back to work in Hastings on Monday afternoon. Dr. F. A Baria was the physician in charge.

Maree with Bobby Deane McNamee

Tragedy struck the young McNamee family in the fall of 1934. Maree had contracted tuberculosis sometime around 1932. According to a PBS documentary, *TB in America:*

1895 – 1954, by the end of the 19th century, tuberculosis or consumption, had killed one in seven of all people that had ever lived. Victims suffered from hacking, bloody coughs, and debilitating pain in their lungs and fatigue. Throughout the 1800s, consumptive patients sought cures in sanatoriums where it was believed that rest and a healthful climate could change the course of the disease.

The Wyoming Tuberculosis Sanitarium (photo courtesy of the Wyoming State Archives) was established in Basin Wyoming in 1921. It was more commonly referred to as the Basin Sanitarium. According to the *Basin Republican-Rustler* newspaper, the building stopped operating as a sanitarium about 1969 and sat empty until 1981. It was finally torn down in 2012. On the grounds where it once stood sits a modern skilled nursing retirement center which is owned and operated by the State of Wyoming.

Charles, Maree, Bobby and Charlotte McNamee

In accordance with Wyoming law at the time, Charles brought Maree to the sanitarium in the hopes of curing her of the terrible disease or perhaps just to ease her pain. Daughter Charlotte Maree (McNamee) Leipold remembers that the photo was taken was the day before Maree was to leave. She vividly remembers everyone being sad.

Death claimed Maree on September 13, 1934 while she was at the facility. She had only been there two days. The *Ord Quiz* later that week noted the Reverend W. C. McCarthy was the minister and Harlan T.

Frazier was in charge of funeral arrangements. Maree is buried in the Ord Cemetery. The paper noted that "Charlotte Maree and Bobby Deane, who are with their father, mourn the untimely death of this tender, loving wife and mother." Also left were Maree's father, two brothers and two sisters. Rose Margaret (McNamee) Rorabeck and Anna Louise (McNamee) Ackerman both drove in from Wyoming to attend the funeral. The newspaper reported that Charles McNamee returned to his employment in Cheyenne, WY. His children, Bobby and Charlotte, remained living in Ord with their grandfather, Henry VanSlyke and family.

Charlotte Maree, Charles, Bobby Deane McNamee

Bobby and Charlotte moved back to Cheyenne after the Christmas holiday. But on June 6, 1935 the newspaper reported that "Charles McNamee and children, Charlotte and Bobby, came Wednesday from Cheyenne, WY to visit in the Henry VanSlyke home. Charlotte and Bobby will stay in Ord during the summer. Charles McNamee returned Friday to Cheyenne."

Bernadine Elsie Lex – Charles McNamee married Bernadine Elsie Lex of Dow, Iowa. The family lore tells us that Bernadine had traveled to Nebraska aboard the bus that Charles drove. At the bus station, Bernadine fell down the stairs and Charles came to her rescue. Their story will continue in another book.

15 RAYMOND THOMAS MCNAMEE

Raymond was born on November 5, 1907 in Richmond, Missouri. It appears that Raymond never married or had children.

On October 16, 1940 Raymond registered for the World War II draft in Casper, Wyoming. He was 5' 10" tall and weighed 154 pounds. He had gray eyes and brown hair. At the time he was living in the Yellowstone Hotel of 204 N. Durbin St. in Casper (which is still operating. See vintage photo from Ebay) and working as a waiter for a Mr. Ralph Fulton at the Rex

Hamburger restaurant which went out of business about 1975.

According *Dobby's Frontier Town*, a website that chronicles old Nebraska, Rex Hamburgers was started in Alliance, Nebraska in 1927 by Rex Meyers. The shop has seven stools and Rex served hamburgers, pie, coffee and milk. Chili was also added to the menu in winter and customers could pick up their favorite candy bar too. The hamburgers sold for a nickel each or six for a quarter. The hamburgers were fried in rendered beef suet and the grill was heated by a Coleman camp stove. Rex then went to Casper Wyoming to open another hamburger shop and while there his partner absconded with all their money so Rex was forced to come back to Alliance and run the shop here.

Raymond entered the Wyoming Army National Guard in Casper, Wyoming on February 24, 1941. He served as a cook and held the rank of Private in the Cavalry. He was single with no dependents. How long he served in the Army National Guard is unknown. He may have been sent to Europe during the War, but this has not been confirmed.

After mustering out of the Army Raymond worked for a time as a waiter in Portland, Oregon before moving to Idaho Falls, Idaho. Raymond died at age 62 in Idaho Falls, Idaho on October 19, 1970. He is buried in Fielding Memorial Park Cemetery in Idaho Falls.

16 WILBUR BRUCE MCNAMEE

Born in Richmond, Missouri, November 10, 1909, Wilbur Bruce was the 10th child of Michael and Anna Maree. He died on May 14, 1971 in Columbus, Ohio. He is buried at the Fernwood Cemetery, in Lockbourne, Ohio, a suburb of Columbus. His last known residence was 43125 Groveport, Franklin, Ohio, USA.

Wilbur first appears in Vinton Valley, Nebraska in the U.S. Census of 1910 where he is simply listed as "Baby" McNamee. The family must have recently moved as "Baby" McNamee's birthplace is listed as Missouri.

Like most young men in America, Wilbur dutifully registered for the World War II draft on October 16, 1940. He was 29 years old at the time and had gone down to the Ord Draft Board with his younger brother Paul McNamee. He listed his employer as the Works Progress Administration. His description showed that he was 5'9" tall, weighed 150 pounds, had gray eyes and brown hair.

On May 28, 1931, the *Ord Quiz* announced that, *"Miss Margaret Fay Cook, daughter of Mr. and Mrs. Parker Cook, and Wilbur McNamee, son of Mr. and Mrs. Mike McNamee, were married last Wednesday evening by Judge J. H. Hollingshead. They will make their home on the place farmed by the groom's father."*

In June, 1931, the Ord Quiz reported, "Mrs. Percy Benson gave a miscellaneous shower for Faye Cook McNamee Friday afternoon at her home. A large number of friends and relatives were guests. Faye received many useful and beautiful presents. The Will Zikmund, Charlie McNamee families, Tom Hanrahan and James McNamee were Sunday visitors in the McNamee home.

Maree Henrietta van slyke, Charles McNamee, possibly Faye Cook, Wilbur McNamee

Mr. and Mrs. Park Cook and Mr. and Mrs. Wilbur McNamee were at Ericson fishing Thursday afternoon."

One note of tragedy: On October 13, 1932 the *Ord Quiz* reported:

"ROLLAND WILBER MCNAMEE — Ord friends and relatives were saddened Saturday evening to learn of the sudden passing of little Rolland Wilber McNamee, son of Mr. and Mrs. Wilber McNamee of the Elm Creek neighborhood. The baby had been ailing about three weeks and a sudden illness of summer diarrhea proved fatal, though he was brought to the doctor Saturday morning. He died at the home of Mr. and Mrs. Will Zikmund in Ord, being 11 months and 18 days old. Last rites were held at the Frazier Chapel Tuesday afternoon with Rev. Real in charge and internment was in Ord Cemetery.

On April 6, 1951, Wilbur was the proud father who gave away his daughter Ellen at her wedding to Frank Chadwick at the Wayne County, Indiana courthouse. Ellen was employed as a key-punch operator. Wilbur listed his occupation as Machinist.

17 PAUL MCNAMEE

The youngest of the 11 children born to Michael and Anna, Paul came into the world in Ord, Nebraska on September 25th, 1912 and, except for a short stint with the Civilian Conservation Corps and a failed attempt to join the U.S. Army, never left the area. He remained single his entire life and produced no known children. Paul died on December 20, 1950 at age 38 of a coronary thrombosis and is buried in the Ord Cemetery.

The 1920 U.S. Federal Census showed six-year-old Paul at home on the farm in Vinton Township, Nebraska with his 10 other siblings.

By the 1930 U.S. Federal Census, most of the McNamee brood had left the nest leaving 17-year-old Paul and his older brothers Wilbur and Raymond to take care of the farm. Since the last census, the family had moved and was then living on a rented farm in Springdale Township, not far from their previous home.

The 1940 U.S. Federal Census showed that Paul lived with his brother Wilbur McNamee. Though he finished 8th grade, he apparently had a tough time finding work. He worked sometimes as a common laborer for an athletic field but was unemployed 48 out of 52 weeks in the previous year. He worked for an undetermined period for Mr. James Sutton, in the town of Tribune, Greeley County, Kansas. It should be noted that all of the previous census surveys estimated Paul's birth year as 1913-1914. But when Paul registered for the draft on October 16, 1940, he listed his actual birthday as September 25, 1912. His World War II draft card described Paul as 5' 5" tall, weighing in at 130 pounds, and with hazel eyes and brown hair. Paul had a distinctive scar on his neck.

In April 1942, Paul was one of the largest Valley County, Nebraska groups of draftees called up for Army service. Assembled and ready by 5:30 a.m. in the morning, 22 young men boarded the bus and departed for a secret camp for evaluation and induction.

Nebraskans were proud to serve in the military and even prouder of their boys who were chosen to go off to war. In honor of the boys, the American Legion, Rotary Club, Cosmopolitan Club and the Ord Chamber of Commerce came together to put on a send-off dinner at Thorne's Cafe in downtown Ord. Afterwards all 22 young men were guests of Mr. and Mrs. E. O. Kull at the Onyx Cafe *"for as long as they cared to stay."* The Onyx Cafe was a popular event space and restaurant that according to an advertisement in the *Ord Quiz*, served "*superbly rare steaks, fried chicken, luscious golden brown French Fries, short orders, and sandwiches.*" Cover charge on Saturday nights was 50 cents. They hosted many a luncheon, dinner party and dances for Ord residents.

The morning the recruits were to leave, the American Legion Auxiliary turned out an impressive array of coffee and donuts for the recruits and any family members that showed up at the bus station to see them off. Paul's service didn't last long though. The following week, he was one of 10 recruits who, according to Virginia Davis, county draft clerk, "*failed to pass their physical examinations for various reasons*" and were rejected by the Army. Paul returned to Ord where he remained for the rest of his life.

The *Ord Quiz* (December 28, 1950) reported that *"Paul McNamee of Ord died suddenly while at work, Wednesday afternoon, December 20, 1950. He was helping with the digging of a cesspool on the Martin Fuss farm when he was stricken. He had died when he was found by several fellow workers.*

Mr. McNamee had been employed by the Rowbal Plumbing Company of Ord since early summer of 1949. He had not complained of any ill health and his sudden passing was completely unexpected.
Funeral services were held Saturday afternoon from the Hastings-Pearson chapel in Ord for Paul who died Wednesday, December 20 at the age of 37 years, 2 months, and 25 days.

The Rev. R. E. Daughetee officiated. Pallbearers were Bob Adamek, Alvin Anderson, Cash Wozniak, Walter Anderson, Vic Welniak, and Eugene Brown.
Paul was the son of Mr. and Mrs. Michael McNamee. He was born Sept. 25, 1913 and was reared in Valley County.

His parents and two brothers, James and Charles, preceded him in death. Survivors include four brothers and four sisters. They are John of Beatrice; Robert of Gothenburg; Raymond of Casper, Wyo; Wilbur of Lockbourne, Ohio; Mrs. Catherine Zikmund of Ord; Mrs. Rose Rorabeck of Mid-West, Wyo; Mrs. Anna Ackerman of Casper, Wyo; and Martha Chilewski of Comstock. Burial was in Graceland, Ord Cemetery."

18 CONCLUSION

The genealogies we create are sometimes called conclusion trees. Each name, date, place, and relationship in the tree is a conclusion, "a decision…based on well-reasoned and thoroughly documented evidence gleaned from sound research." I don't claim proficiency, just a keen interest to know the facts and stories as best I could and to share them with others.

What you are holding is not a complete work. In fact, it is just the beginning of a portrait of an American family. My hope is that it sheds some light for you, brings you some joy, and even inspires you to jump in and do some research on your own.

ABOUT THE AUTHOR

David McNamee, Ph.D. is the oldest of the six children born to Bobby Deane and Ruth Evelyn (Winberg) McNamee. Proud to count himself a "military brat," he went on to his own career in the U.S. Air Force followed by a long stint as a college professor and university administrator (a career from which he is still recovering). He is married to Lynne E. McNamee, who had her own distinguished Air Force career. They are blessed with two grown sons, Christopher Joseph and Daniel Garrick McNamee, who are blazing their own unique paths in the world.